# In my Heart, A Volcano

# In my Heart, A Volcano

## by Rhina Mercedes
A translation from the Spanish by David Vine

## RIOT OF ROSES
### PUBLISHING HOUSE
SEJATNGA
UNCEDED TONGVA TERRITORY
SOUTH WHITTIER, CALIFORNIA

Published by Riot of Roses Publishing House

In My Heart, A Volcano: *A Memoir in Vignettes*

Copyright © 2025, Rhina Mercedes Ramos
ISBN (paperback): 978-1-961717-35-0
ISBN (ebook): 978-1-961717-36-7

Translated by *David Vine*
Edited by *Margaret M. Robinson*
Graphic Design by *Pedro José Durán* and *Mariana Guadalupe Guzmán*
Photography from the author's personal archives

Cover Artist© Pedro José Durán and Mariana Guadalupe Guzmán, 2025

Primera edición en español:
Museo de la Palabra y la Imagen
San Salvador, 2025
Publisher: Carlos Henríquez Consalvi
Museo de la Palabra y la Imagen (MUPI)
27.a Av. Norte, #1140, Urb. La Esperanza
San Salvador, El Salvador.
Tel.: +(503) 2564-7005
www.museo.com.sv

To request permissions, you may contact the Publisher at riotofrosesllc@gmail.com. For bookings and interviews, contact the author at rhinamercedesramos@gmail.com

Printed in the United States of America.
www.riotofrosespublishinghouse.com
Cover design by waseem@arrowupz.com
Layout design by waseem@arrowupz.com
Editor-in-Chief Brenda Vaca

*To Shinobu, for encouraging all my dreams.*

# Table of Contents

# Introduction

Tangled in the roots of a little girl's memory--a little girl who wanted to be an angel--twine those of her personal story and that of her family. Growing, green, living roots. Roots that spread beyond borders, into other cultures and other languages.

At the beginning of this book, we are introduced to a magical world in which a mere glance from Uncle Ermenegildo can put a scorpion to sleep and tame any beast grazing in in the pastures of a child's universe. Where Grandmother Rosa, bearing the weight of eternal guilt, warns of the *Eye of God*, an eye that stalks us throughout the day, and asserts that you must eat everything on your plate because your guardian angel is watching like a hawk.

This is an imaginary world in which good and evil are locked in eternal battle, a place patrolled by dwarves dressed as colonial pilgrims, who terrified a good little girl, falsely accusing her of having torn up a photograph of the Pope. Rhina Mercedes' memories speak to us of a young teenager forced to move north, to live in a multicolored crucible of experiences, of sorrows and joys. Her mind ever trained on her native soil, it must not have been easy living with a volcano in her heart.

Rhina Mercedes paints for us a picture of the world and the lives of numerous women who, in their peregrinations, forded rivers of exclusion, crossed human deserts, overcame a thousand obstacles, defied social stigmas and stoically survived in foreign lands.

She recounts for us both the geographical journeys and the internal voyages that shaped her identity. She undoes he compacted knots of silence to give voice to the many Salvadoran women and girls who have been denied the right to communicate, to tell their stories.

Thank you, Rhina, for your courage. Thank you for showing us that our strength is in our diversity. Thank you for working to create, along with other girls and women, that world of which we have dreamed, a world in which all things are possible. Thank you for your words!

*Carlos Henríquez Consalvi, Santiago*

# What Am I
# About to Tell You?

The fairy tales and scary stories of my youth were the narratives about my family. Grandmothers who ceaselessly prayed interminable rosaries. Poet grandfathers who, though illiterate, composed verses with the purpose of making women fall in love. Uncles who could put scorpions to sleep and kill goats with no more than a glance. These stories, mixed with my own imagination, brewed a perfect magic for my childhood world. I listened attentively to the stories told around me. Some of the details, however, were incomplete, some secrets unspoken, some truths silently accepted. Because of those, this story will at times reflect my personal deductions.

I wish to tell the story that paved my path and shaped the direction of the new generations of my nieces and nephews, and of others, too, who have been affected here and there by the love and the sorrow of the ones who came before us. These are stories of family, of pain and of hope. These images and words could rest no longer in my head, but had to burst out onto paper, having yearned, for decades, to be roaming freely across the page.

# Looks
## That Kill

Scorpions detect their victims by the vibrations that the latter produce. They can sense the skittering of a cockroach over a foot and half away. My uncle Ermenegildo could put scorpions to sleep with a mere glance. He would look at them and the little critters flipped over and were said to fall into a dream state, belly up.

Once Tío Mere took down a goat by turning his eyes to it. Its owner had refused him permission to pet the little kid. My aunt María, who had witnessed the scene, thought to herself, "This woman has no idea what's about to hit her." The mighty glance of Tío Mere went into action and he toppled the goat without meaning to. His gifted vision, however, could not save him from alcohol. That thirst of his for liquor was unquenchable! It led him to the grave at the age of forty, entirely spent.

My mother claims to possess a potent glance as well. According to her, the foam will not rise on eggs if she looks at them while she is beating them. Personally, I prefer my uncle's magic power to my mother's culinary calamity.

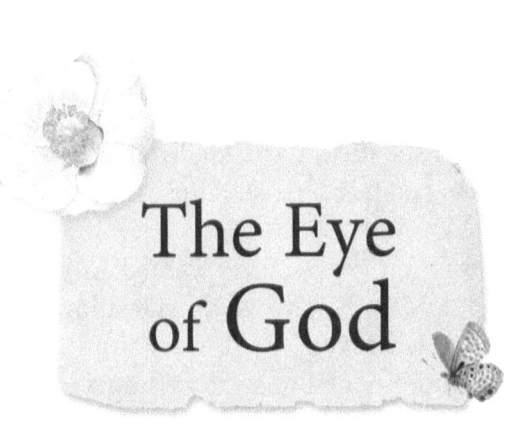

# The Eye
## of God

My grandmother, Mamá Rosa, strove to become an angel. When she died, I was finally able to write my first story, free at last from her stalking eyes.

When I was ten years old, I wanted to begin keeping a diary, but Mamá Rosa would not allow it. Her eyes followed me wherever I went every time I snatched my notebook and a pencil to start writing about the things that were going on around me. All I wanted to do was write about the people I saw, the sunrises, the volcano that loomed in front of me when the door was opened from inside the place where I grew up in El Salvador. Mamá Rosa was unceasingly aware of my every movement, just as was the ever-present *Eye of God*. She used to tell me that there was an eye that tracked us throughout the day. It was the **Ojo de Dios** and could see everything we did. I imagined an enormous eyeball hanging from the ceiling.

Mamá Rosa also had me convinced that I had to eat everything on my plate because my guardian angel was keeping an eye on me, and he would get sad if I didn't finish all my food. That's why I ate up all those plates, loaded with food, that Abuelita—as we called her—put in front of me. That damned guardian angel! He never got fat. But I did, and at the age of ten I was already an obese child. I would eat ten tortillas and a whole sardine just to keep the angel happy.

My grandmother's gaze was penetrating, just like that of my uncle Mere, who could put scorpions to sleep. Behind the thick lenses of her glasses, her eyes could reach the corners where I hid in order to play or write. I remember that I kept my diary on my person for a whole week so she couldn't read it. But eventually, I tired of hiding. One fine day, I went into the bathroom, tore out the pages of the notebook one by one, and threw them down the toilet. I "disappeared" the evidence that thoughts captured on paper possess the power to make someone shake in their boots, that words can form images in the minds of those who can bring them to life. Doubtless, Mamá Rosa was afraid of my thoughts. She imagined—because she said it to me repeatedly—that my head was full of lustful and sinful images. "Lust" and "sin" were among the first words I learned as a little child, thanks to the fact that Mamá Rosa accused me at every turn of being in the act of something of that sort. In my childhood I learned that women are possessed of a sinful nature, because, according to my grandmother, women lead others to sin. Women are guilty of Original Sin, since Eve gave Adam the apple, and that is where everything got screwed up.

Mamá Rosa accused me of having torn the photograph of the Pope that she jealously guarded in her wardrobe. I swore that it hadn't been me. The photo already had a tiny tear on one corner, but in her sanctimonious eyes, I was responsible for whatever went wrong. If I defended myself, she refused to believe me. So, it was easier just to let her think that I was capable of any wicked deed.

She believed I was an evil girl. Now that I am an adult, it seems incredible to me that she could have thought that, because I was the granddaughter who most observed her teachings about good and evil, about God and the Devil, about heaven and hell. When I was about six years old, I remember, I heard a group of older boys criticizing the Catholic church. They were behind our apartment discussing why they wouldn't confess to a Catholic priest. Bottom line, they were saying, a priest is just a human being like anyone else. I was shocked by what they were suggesting, and I ran to where my grandmother was doing housework, and told her, "Mamá Rosa, there are some boys out there who don't believe in God." Mamá Rosa grabbed a washbasin full of water and threw it out the window at the boys, shouting at them, "Heretics! Jews! Beat it, you heretics!" The Inquisition had its messenger in the middle of the twentieth century, my grandmother Rosa. And I was her assistant. Together we persecuted heretics and applied punishment by water to those who dared question the priests.

In addition to the torn photo of the Pope, in my grandmother's wardrobe there were no end of saints, relics, Virgins and crucifixes. These symbols were her companions, morning, noon and night. Invoking them non-stop, she used to pray:

*Holy Mary, Mother of God, pray for us sinners now and at the hour of our death... I believe in God the Father Almighty, in the resurrection of the body and in life everlasting. Amen.*

When Mamá Rosa would open the doors of her wardrobe, there appeared the martyrs of the Christian faith. There was a certain Saint Sebastian, stuck all over with arrows and writhing in pain. There was Saint Martin de Porres, a black saint who had been a slave and carried a broom. He had acquired his sainthood in return for suffering the humiliations visited on him by the white Spanish priests. Also in the wardrobe was a saint called *Judas Tadeo[1]* who got me very confused since, just ten years old, I did not understand that there was a Judas who could have been a saint. Wasn't Judas the man who betrayed Jesus? But I never dared ask Mamá Rosa about that. She would have thought I wanted to start a cult of Judas the traitor.

Mamá Rosa with grandson Paquito who died in infancy.

---

[1] English makes a distinction between *Judas* Iscariot, the betrayer of Jesus, and Saint *Jude* Thaddeus, one of the Twelve Apostles. Both men are called *Judas* in Spanish.

The saint who really terrified me was the Holy Child of Atocha. This saint was a dwarf dressed like a Colonial pilgrim, in a floor-length black robe, wearing a black Quaker's hat, with red lips, pasty skin and black curls that hung down on both sides from the hat. In the two upper corners of his icon were scenes in which miracles were being performed through his divine intervention. In one of the scenes the Child of Atocha was shown saving a woman who was being stabbed to death. In the other image was a sick man on his death bed, being healed by the Child. This saint always scared me stiff because he looked like a child ghost. I wouldn't have called upon *him* to save me for anything in the world!

These were the witnesses before whom my grandmother petitioned heaven, begging them to make her an angel. Was that why her full name was Rosenda *Ángela* Majano Coreas? Perhaps she thought that, by fervently appealing to them, she could be rid of carnal thoughts with which she was tormented her whole life. Abuela believed that the flesh was lustful, that with the body one could nothing but evil. Mamá Rosa didn't want to feel the sensations of her body, so she lashed herself when she prayed the rosary. Once I saw her flagellating herself with the inner tube of a bicycle tire. She was thrashing her back as she recited her prayers. She struggled with guilt. She always fought the guilt she felt over the fact that she was a "sinful" woman. Surely it had to have been her sexual fantasies that drove her to chant endlessly her long litanies:

> *Tower of Ivory, pray for us.*
> *Star of the morning, pray for us.*

And sometimes she even prayed these litanies in Latin, which was exceedingly strange because at that point she could neither read nor write. She only learned to read around the age of fifty, and from then on never read another book but the Bible. The Catholic Church and unceasing prayer were the two most important things to her. A day did not pass on which she didn't light her candles in preparation for praying her interminable rosaries. She made me and my brother pray the rosary before we could go out to play. We developed incredible speed at it, so we could finish the prayer and go out to the street. I don't know how we did it, but our Lord's Prayers practically came out as tongue-twisters!

It was said that at one point, Abuela had accrued a lot of debt on account of having financially helped the church in her town. In her desperation, she went and lay down on the railroad tracks because she wanted to die. My mother convinced her to get up so the train wouldn't crush her, and helped her pay the money that she had come to owe as a result of her faith.

Mamá Rosa usually prayed, too, for the main characters of her soap operas to be happy. She loved watching the telenovelas. (And so do I!). When Mamá Rosa saw the actors on the shows crying and suffering, she worried terribly and prayed her rosaries even more intensely. Abuela was quite surprised when these actors would reappear in the role of a new character on another telenovela. But she was glad to see them again. And you might say that she really was the one responsible for the repeated reincarnations of the actors Verónica Castro and Lucía Méndez.

They tell me that my grandmother's fear of (and perhaps her appetite for) sex began when a man took her, at the age of seventeen, "up the mountain" to make her a woman. In El Salvador a girl does not become a woman until a man "takes" her. As if she were livestock that must be branded.

Mamá Rosa had been orphaned at the age of six and to survive, she began serving in the homes of the wealthy in her town. She told me that she was so little when she started working as a servant, her employers had to stack up bricks for her to stand on so that she could reach the sink. Abuela had no one to protect her when was growing up. It is easy to image that someone could take her by force to rape her. She went without many things during her childhood. She had no education, no food, not even a secure place to live. That experience made her vigilant that nothing edible was ever thrown in the trash. When it came to leftovers she always said, "Better it should cause harm than that it should be wasted."

Mamá Rosa married my grandfather Alfonso, with whom she lived "in sin," as she was given to say, for more than fifty years. Abuelo had been wed before, so the priest would not let them marry in the Church. Perhaps that's why Abuela had to spend so many afternoons in prayer, why she had to pray in public out in front of the building where we lived in El Salvador. Our neighbors thought that Mamá Rosa was crazy. What those others didn't know was that my grandmother was desperate to be an angel. Or at least to stop being a woman.

# The Last
# Purebred

I know very little about the life of my grandmother Menche, my father's mother. But according to my cousin Katia, Abuela, born Mercedes Cortez, was the product of a scandal. A family of Spanish descent, not yet mixed with persons of indigenous blood, had a son who chose to get involved with my great-grandmother, and from their union came Abuela Mercedes. Of course, in addition to her status as a half-breed, my grandmother inherited nothing else.

She was a woman not to be messed with. She kept a stall in the market from which she often stocked the pantry at our house. She was a generous but exacting woman. They say that she had left my grandfather Andrés because he was a drunk, a womanizer and an abuser.

When he was quite small, my father was put under the care of his older sisters. My dad told me that he only met his mom for the first time when he was around five years old and that he had trouble seeing her as his mother. It was my aunt Ofelia, his older sister, who took care of him like a son. During his childhood, she raised him and his sister Tía Vicky as well.

Abuela Menche, as we called her, came to visit us as often as she could, and fretted over us more than she ever had over my father. She helped my mom with whatever she could--oil, rice, beans. I was afraid of her, though, because she seemed to be angry all the time. But my cousin Katia tells me that she was actually very sweet and dedicated to her grandchildren. I bear her name, Mercedes, as my middle name. Many of her other granddaughters were also named Mercedes. Being one of the eldest of them, however, my father's family called me *La Menchota*, "Big Menche." I hated that they referred to me that way and repeatedly said, "My name is Rhina." When I had the opportunity to shed my middle name, though, I chose not to because I understood that it was a good thing to respect that part of my heritage. Now I am very proud to say that name is Rhina Mercedes.

# Women Who
# Clip Wings

Photo of Tía María at the age of 18

In my grandmother Rosa's world, a man had more value than a woman. She really spoiled her male children. She gave them whatever they wanted. But, with her daughters, Mamá Rosa was utterly tyrannical, to the point––to say the least––that she forbade my aunt María to go to school in another town.

Tía María was very intelligent, so they say. She could even draw maps, very skillfully, from memory. The young schoolgirl had won a scholarship to study to become a teacher. But my grandmother objected that, if she left for another town, it wouldn't be long before she came back pregnant. "Boss lady" would not consent, thus quashing her dream of studying for a career that would get her ahead.

Abuela was so despotic, Tía María tells me, that when she sent María to the river to fetch water, she would threaten, "I am going to spit on the ground, and you had better be back before the spittle dries. Because if you're not, you're going to be dealing with me."

Faced with an ultimatum like that, the young girl was off like a shot down to the stream, skittering like a three-legged dog,[2] tripping over branches, stones, whatever, in order to get back before the damned spittle evaporated from the floor.

Since she was a little girl, Tía María has found delight in flowers, has always adored them. She recounts that she was particularly drawn to cutting some white flowers that grew in a neighbor lady's garden. Whenever she got back home, overjoyed with the blossoms, and Mamá Rosa found them, then would come the punishment! She always had to hide them, because if Abuelita saw them, there would be a price to pay. And the punishment always came in the form of beatings. My aunt doesn't know why my grandmother was so merciless and cruel toward her, but despite being punished for it each time, Tía María still enjoyed the sweet pleasure of having picked those flowers. Now that my aunt María can no longer walk, she loves admiring the flowers that my cousin Lupita planted for her on the patio where she lives. She is fond of changing them from flowerpot to flowerpot and to watering them, like if in doing so she is healing her soul.

"I don't know why she did those things to me," Tía María says. And *I* don't understand either. The truth is that Abuela didn't know how to be a mother. The most likely explanation for that is that her harshness of her childhood, the vulnerability made her like that. She lacked any knowledge of what tenderness was. And after suffering unimaginable abuses, she grew to hate living in a woman's body. She was simply unable to give

---

[2] Sp., like a chucha cuta. A Salvadorean expression, literally, a "crippled bitch."

her daughters the love she never had. And perhaps, recognizing that men wielded more power, she ceded them all her obeisance.

There are women who internalize the rejection that this world offers them just for being women. Consequently, they turn into the cruelest of jailers. Without the resources or the support necessary to take flight themselves, they clip the wings of other women.

# The Tragic Lives of the Males in My Family

My uncle Virgilio, whom I never met, was a merchant. He had a history of personal run-ins. From the looks of it, some of his antagonists tried to rob him and he ended up dead, decapitated with a machete. It is rumored that it was his own brothers-in-law who were trying to get revenge on him, and it was one of them who murdered him.

The day they beheaded Tío Virgilio, my grandmother, Mamá Rosa, was in church at Mass. She was always either at Mass or praying at home. Tía María tells it that, on that day, a black dog entered the church and lay down at Abuela Rosa's feet. They say that, upon seeing the dog, Mamá Rosa ran to where her son's body had been laid out and, raising her hands to heaven, petitioned God to punish his murderers with death. But she also importuned God that he forgive them. Her initial petition was heard, because my aunt María says that Tío Virgilio's murderer was found hacked to pieces with a machete exactly seven months and four days after my uncle was beheaded. In this town of my aunt's there was a lot of violence. People killed each other as if it were nothing. And my aunt says that every weekend saw two men dead over quarrels.

Another uncle of mine, Tío Mere, expired drooling, surely destroyed internally because he drank every day. Alcohol was his God.

My uncle Toño died alone at the age of seventy from a heart attack. He was found a couple of days after, lying on the floor of our apartment in San Salvador. When Tío Toño was young, he abandoned all his children without a concern as to whether they had food, shelter or got an education. He was such a heartless man that, while still young, he asked my grandparents for his inheritance so he could leave home. Eventually, my grandmother, who had not seen him for a long time, even prayed a *novenario*[3] for him because she believed him to be dead. But, as the song goes: *He wasn't dead, he was out partying*[4].

When he grew old, none of his children wanted to take care of him. My mother gave *him* a place to live, our apartment in San Salvador, and he died there all alone. My aunt María tells how he used to beat her savagely when they were young if she hadn't ironed his clothes the way he wanted, or just to vent his rage on her. Tía María says that once my uncle shot a gun at her feet (fortunately, she was not injured) because she hadn't cooked his egg just the way he liked it. At one point, my mother jumped on my uncle's back and squeezed him by the neck and, my aunt María says, together they gave

---

[3] A nine-day period of prayers of grief, mourning and bereavement for a deceased loved one.
[4] *No estaba muerto, andaba de parranda*. Los Cañameros, 2013.

him a beating that left him disinclined to harass them anymore. Even so, at age of eighteen my aunt had to flee the constant mistreatment. She left home to work in local shops. She preferred to be alone rather than go on enduring physical abuse at the hands of my uncle and my grandmother.

All my uncles were irresponsible, womanizers, drunks and troublemakers. Their profusion of sons and daughters were left without protection, left to their own fates from when they were very small. It was my mother and Tía María and Mamá Rosa who took charge of raising some of my cousins who had nothing to eat, no place to live and no means of attending school. My aunt tells me that she made clothes for them out of her own skirts. That was how she learned the art of the seamstress. My cousin Luis remembers with great sorrow that, when he was just a tiny boy, his mother gave him and his siblings away like puppies to the rest of the family, to whichever of them were able to take them in and support them.

The most fitting anthem I can dedicate to those men, who are not the exception but the rule in countries like El Salvador, is the song written by José María Napoleón defining true manliness:

*You're not more of a man just because you look like one / Or because you can shout louder and be scarier / But if your word is your bond / You're not more of a man just because you have more women / Or because you drink more and can hold it / But if you have only one woman and you only drink to quench your thirst.[5]*

---

[5] *No es más hombre el que parece / Ni el que grita más y espanta /Sino el que tiene en su voz la verdad de su palabra / Ni el que tiene más mujeres / Ni el que bebe más y aguanta / Sino el que tiene una sola y una sed para calmarla. Hombre.* José María Napoleón, 2015.

# I Am Only
# Six Years Old

When I was six years old, one of my older male cousins, who had been raised with us, sexually abused me. He was eighteen, and had started abusing me when they let him babysit me. While Abuelita was doing laundry or household chores, he would touch me and make me touch him. And, as I remember it, on one occasion there was penetration. His sexual abuse caused me to develop an infection. They took me to the doctor and that was how they found out what had happened to me. After conducting a few tests, the doctor sat me on the examination table and asked me, "Does someone touch you?" I recall answering, with the innocence of a little girl, "Yes, my cousin Morita touches me." The doctor went immediately into another room where my mother was waiting and spoke with her. I didn't hear any of the conversation about me. I only remember that my mother came to get me so that we could go home. She didn't speak a word to me, she just took me by the hand. Her face was sad. On the bus, I could see that she was crying. But she didn't say anything. She just put me in an empty seat and stood next to me. That journey in deafening silence resulted in a great wound that was only healed over the course of my life. I wanted to know what was happening and why my mama's eyes were fixed on empty space and not on me.

When we got home, she and my aunt María went into my mother's bedroom and shut the door. After a while behind the closed door, they summoned me. I went into the room, and they began interrogating me. My aunt asked me, "Why didn't you say anything?" I didn't answer. I didn't know what was happening and I didn't realize that I was being accused of something or what it was that I had done wrong. My aunt was very angry and shouted at me, "You didn't say anything because you liked it!" Again, I didn't reply. What could a six-year-old child say regarding something she didn't know anything about?

After the abuse came to light, my mother began giving me injections and administering suppositories. She never said what they were for. I only remember that they hurt. I was afraid of needles and at times she had to chase me around the apartment so get me to let her inject me. Nobody ever sat down with me and explained what was happening to my body and why they were treating me so roughly and looked at me so angrily. I began to experience an immense feeling of guilt.

Because she was very superstitious and believed in spirits, my aunt decided to seek out the help of medicine men. Her aim was to exorcise the demons she thought had possessed me. I remember one of those visits to a medicine man. In a dark room lit by candles my aunt and the gentleman with whom she was consulting regarded me and spoke to one another. He recommended that she give me bitter rue baths. The next day, my aunt went to cut (steal) rue from a neighbor's yard. Then she steeped the herb and gave me the bath. I remember vaguely that she repeated some words as she bathed me. They say that the psychic qualities of rue are the effects of warding off negative energy and purifying the mind. I didn't understand anything at all about what those treatments were for--the rue, the supplications, the accusatory looks. There I was, the focus of all that boundless attention designed to heal me, save me, cleanse me. And nobody was explaining to me what was going on. The world can be an overwhelming place when you are little, and the grownups only communicate with one another or within their own heads.

Although I didn't know exactly what I had done wrong, I started to be ashamed of my body and to feel dirty. The images of what my cousin had done to me replayed in my mind and at times wouldn't stop, like a movie that wouldn't end. In my catechism classes, in preparation for my first communion, I had already learned how to sign myself with the cross, so, every time those memories came to my mind, I signed myself compulsively. Time and time again I signed myself with the cross in an effort to get those filthy thoughts out of my head. If making the sign of the cross had been an Olympic sport, I would have gotten a silver medal, at least! I spat too, constantly, because I felt disgust. I don't know how a such a little girl, so deeply sensitive, and with a photographic memory to boot, ever managed to grow up, while crossing herself thousands of times a day! I stopped signing myself so bizarrely, so compulsively one day when a young girl at my school, older than I was, asked me if I was feeling okay or if something was wrong. That's when I stopped performing my cleansing ritual, to avoid drawing attention to myself.

Now that I am an adult, my mother tells me that the doctor told her not to discuss the incident with me because, since I was so little, I would surely forget about it on my own. But, since the adults in my life, rather than console me, were making me feel guilty, how was I going to forget? Sometimes a child is the salvation of grownups who are unwilling to own up to their failures and want of responsibility. That abuse shattered my innocence and marked my life.

When they told Mamá Rosa about the abuse, she too concluded that it had been my fault. I think that is why she was hypervigilant around me all the time, why she decided that it was I who had torn the photograph of the Pope. I was the thing she feared most. But maybe, just like my grandmother, I too wanted to cease being a woman and become an angel. How similar and yet how different we were, Mamá Rosa and I, because we had each been irreparably harmed in our childhoods.

My cousin was kicked out and never showed his face again at our house. This incident became a well-guarded family secret, only discussed in whispers with glances in my direction. Once I heard someone say that, if they told my dad, he might kill my cousin Morita. Our family was full of these kinds of secrets. Without venturing into any more of them, suffice it to say that in my family story many "characters" are lurking still, the ghosts of our lives.

Over the years, my imperfect family and I have healed the wounds. But a wound is something that scars. It leaves the marks of suffering not only on the skin but in the soul. In the end, time, a good dose of love, people who listen to us--these are the never-failing medicines for the invisible wounds. Reclaiming the body after abuse is a daily struggle to get back into our former skin, the skin that was taken away from us. Nowadays, I work with an exercise trainer. In addition to showing me how to improve my balance, she has taught me to reclaim my body by lifting weights, performing daily routines that help me understand that this is *my* body, no one else's.

Once, as an adult, I tried to share what had happened to me with my father, but he immediately asked me to stop. He said, "Please, don't tell me!" Years later, he confessed that he had shushed me because he was afraid to hear my pain, afraid that *he* would feel guilty. There it was. That guilt. Well, it was I who had borne it for most of my life! My old man would have done well to hear me out and shoulder it with me, though just a bit, that heavy yoke, the burden of believing that I myself had caused the abuse. Once again, I was left alone to serve my sentence, because my father preferred to save himself from his *own* guilt.

The year he died, he expressed a desire to know more about me. We spoke about the subject, and I told him that when I had tried to share it with him, all I had wanted was for him to know me better. By finally hearing me, my father died knowing me that little bit better. And although it was not easy, because I know that he loved me in his own way, it brought us into a more honest relationship than the one we had had for many years.

# Andrés Who Lived on the Street

My grandfather Andrés, my dad's father, was another of my family's mythical characters. He had been a waif and an orphan, just like Mamá Rosa. A little boy as sweet as soft coconut candy, frisky like a spinning top, a tiny tyke who rushes out to play barefoot, a child who like the rain delights in making puddles and splashing in the mud. But that little boy was all alone. Alone like a solitary wave in an immense ocean, like a puff of cloud brushing by a mountain. As alone as a tiny drop in a rushing torrent. As alone as is the early-morning frost before the world wakes up.

He was all of six years old and had no *mama* or *papa*. Poverty had made away with them. Andrés was a child of the streets. For a while, one of his sisters took him in to help him. But her husband forced her to get rid of the youngster because he was getting in the way a lot. So she had to send him back out onto the streets.

Andrés began living on handouts, on whatever he could find discarded on the sidewalk or in  garbage pails. He slept wherever he happened to be when night fell, and many of those nights he spent shivering, unprotected, sick, abandoned.

Left to his fate, on one occasion, as he wandered about, a good man brought him to his house and offered him shelter. Andrés elicited tenderness, as all children do. The man's wife, however, wouldn't tolerate her husband taking in a boy from the streets. She protested, saying, "We're too many as it is ourselves, and haven't enough to eat." So, once again, Andrés had to go, to wander aimlessly, just surviving and striving to understand why it was that he had no home in a world of grownups who seemed to feel no compassion for him.

He became a bagger at a public market and made a few pennies bringing customers their bags of food, fruit, bread, cheese and other groceries. How he wanted to try those oranges, those mangos he was carrying in his little hands! But the weight of the load on his back was a reminder to him that those things were not his. It was a fantasy to think that he could taste those watermelons and cantaloupes that looked so delicious.

As soon as Andrés learned to ride a bicycle, he got work as a bread delivery boy. On one occasion, he lost his balance on the bike. All his bread ended up on the ground. He thought he was a goner. The lad was so afraid to go back to his boss that he left his wares on the ground where they were, and the bicycle too! He himself recounted the story to me, smiling as if it was it was an act of naughtiness that was still fresh in his memory, that he was recalling with nostalgia eighty years after. He told me about this incident like a child telling a story in which the main character comes away triumphant because he has avoided getting caught.

Later on, he got into other work consisting of offering home "funerary" services. People were in the habit of stocking the stone reservoirs with small fish when they went to fetch water--a popular method of escaping the discomfort of awful swarms of mosquitos, and of combatting malaria at the same time. The little finned critters happily devoured all kinds of insect larvae, so people were able to pass their days unbothered in their homes. Andrés would go by their houses, removing any deceased fishes floating motionless in the reservoirs. Afterward, he would restock them with more brightly colored fish that, with a swish of the tail, set to efficiently fulfilling their duties. Andrés watched them and took extra care with them. The fish had a place to swim at their leisure and food to eat. Like them, the boy yearned for a place to live and be nurtured. He adored this job because the little fish he tossed into the troughs were his friends and playmates, and because he was in love with color.

At the age of fourteen, Andrés discovered his calling as a designer of glazed tiles and mosaics. Actually, his first job was as a brick maker. Later, though, he ventured into fashioning tiles. His productions were so beautiful that he even received awards that recognized his unique method of combining colors. Such acknowledgments led him into creating thousands of mosaics that wound up adorning the rooms of wealthy homes. My grandfather Andrés worked for "El Granito" brickworks in the San Jacinto neighborhood for half a century.

Abuelo Andrés taught himself to read and write. He devoured poetry and could tell the most beautiful and saddest love stories, like the story of the Queen of Sheba and King Solomon. The sovereign queen had traveled through those blazing deserts--though but once--just to be with the wise and highly-regarded monarch. So Abuelo Andrés told me. He was an incurable romantic!

Once he shared with me some love poems that he had scribbled for a sweetheart who had broken his heart. She was much younger than he and ended up abandoning him. The bitter bard sang:

*Neida, why? Why did you never tell me that your love was*
*only an illusion,*
*just as is the many-colored rainbow in the heavens?*
*Ah, if you only knew, my love,*
*how dreadful is my desperation!*
*This all-encompassing bitterness!*
*Ah, this emptiness immeasurable and bottomless!*
*When this old clock of mine announces noon,*
*Up and down the street I go, searching, full of hope that I*
*will spy your sweetest form.*
*But all I find is that same emptiness, that awful loneliness.*
*The passersby, they come and go, uninterested in my pain.*
*That is when the weight of it starts to dawn on me,*
*The devastating truth: I am alone. And miserable.*
*So miserable.*
*I make my way to the comedor[6] where so often I used to*
*order for two*
*then come back home, so happy, to you where you were*
*waiting for me with*
*your distinctive smile and a kiss.*

---

[6] Literally "dining room," a humble eatery serving homespun food to the general public.

*That was always the first delicacy that I savored*
*with my burning lips*
*that now pronounce your name today, so thirsty for your*
*love.*
*Ah, Neida! My own Neida!*
*Why—oh why—did you leave without saying goodbye?*

Abuelo also told me that he had invented his own last name. His actual legal name would have been Andrés Sánchez Martínez, and not Andrés Rodríguez, the name by which he identified himself throughout his life. He explained that he assumed the surname "Rodríguez" because, the first time he was asked to give his name, since he was ignorant of it, he replied, "I don't know what my name is. But my father's name was "Rodrigo," so I will be Andrés Rodríguez.[7]

My father told me that Abuelo Andrés was one of the first members of the communist party in El Salvador and that he was known by the nickname *Comandante Sol*, "Commander Sun."

Abuelito Andrés told me all of these marvelous, sometimes sad stories about his childhood as an orphan on the streets of San Salvador one afternoon when we had lunch together in 1992. I promised myself I would write them down someday so as never to forget his history, which is the story of many orphaned children.

---

[7] Originally, in Spanish, *-ez* was a patronymic ending added to a father's first name to create a surname in the pattern "son of.." Names like Álvarez (son of Álvaro), Martínez (son of Martín, González (son of Gonzalo) follow this model. Hence, Rodríguez, "son of Rodrigo." Spanish surnames ending in *-ez* have for many centuries been fossilized in form and no longer relate directly to the given name of the bearer's male parent.

José Orlando Rodríguez (Rhina's father), 1968, while a
student at the teacher training college.

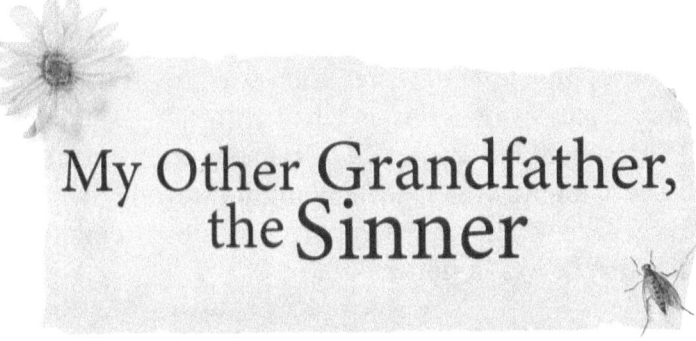

# My Other Grandfather, the Sinner

I also know very little about my grandfather Alfonso, my mother's father. I never got to hear his life story from his own lips as I had with my grandfather Andrés. But I did learn of his escapades as a womanizer, because Mamá Rosa made a point of throwing them up to his face whenever the opportunity arose, reminding him that he was "a sinner."

They say that once he was robbed of some pigs that he had been taking to the market to sell. He had tied them to a post, well secured, and, without a care, had gone into an establishment where certain uncontrollable masculine urges could be quelled. It was one of those houses where they lower men's pants in order to raise their spirits. The brothel sported the name of a very popular analgesic at the time called La Mejoral.[8]

Later, upon exiting La Mejoral, he found the hogs no longer there. Someone had let them off the tether! He, at least, had managed to give free rein to the carnal passions that my grandmother had long since ceased satisfying.

---

[8] A play on words. *La Mejoral* was an analgesic in pill form, advertised as effective against headache, muscular ache, sore throat and a host of other bodily complaints. The name contains the Spanish word *mejor*, "the best," and evokes the popular English quip, "It's good (best) for what ails you."

Mamá Rosa had taken to eating raw onions so that Abuelito Alfonso would not come near her. Poor Mamá Rosa! She gave birth so many times, but several of her children died in infancy. Only five of them survived.

Although Abuelo Alfonso was illiterate, he used to memorize popular songs and trumpet them at the top of his lungs. One of the little tunes he used to sing went like this, "My spoiled little love, when will Sunday come so that I can see you again?" Another went, "Pinto beans, red beans... Oh how they suffer, those who are in love."[9]

They say he was such a womanizer that, the Siguanaba herself appeared to him. According to our folklore, the Siguanaba is a mythological figure who takes the form of a nude, disheveled woman with large breasts who appears to men who have been unfaithful. Legend has it that she was once an indigenous woman of noble birth who, having committed infidelity herself, was condemned to become a monster. I rather think, though, that the Siguanaba was first invented by men aimed at controlling the behavior of women.

My mother took care of my grandfather Alfonso until the end of his days. She says that his death was a peaceful one. I imagine it was. He was so happy-go-lucky! He never seemed to be distressed by anything. He always had some verse to recite or a song to belt out. He was always whistling... Whistling without a care in the world![10]

---

[9] This line rhymes in the original Spanish: *Frijoles pintos, frijoles morados, ¡ay cómo sufren los enamorados!*
[10] *Chiflando en la loma,* a saying that refers to blissfully doing something as if no one were paying attention.

55

# The Town
# Nurse

My mother also took care of Mamá Rosa until her last breath. Being a nurse made it easier for my mom to care for her parents. My aunt sent money, while my mother went physically to El Salvador and stayed for long periods of time to care for my grandparents in their final years.

When Mamá Rosa died, my mother fell into an abyss of sadness. She says that she felt she had become an orphan in this world. During my grandmother's wake, a butterfly fluttered in and alit on my mother. She petted it very gently and tenderly, and the butterfly didn't budge. It sat there, still. Perhaps it was Mamá Rosa's spirit that had finally transformed itself into something that could fly and be free.

My mother and I butted heads when I was a young woman, but over the course of many years, she was my hero. When I was little, I thought my mother was capable of any feat, that she was not afraid of anything or anyone. Of all Mamá Rosa's children, she was the only one who forged a career for herself and escaped my grandmother's severity.

Although my grandparents never approved, my mom advanced in her studies through her own efforts. To matriculate, she sought out women from the neighborhood to accompany her to school and pretend to be her mother so she could register. That's how she managed to finish elementary school.

At that time, matriculating and studying in a rural region wasn't as complicated as it is today. I came across some of her school certificates and discovered that, during elementary school, there were at least two years when she didn't attend. The dates on the certificates confirm that she went back later to finish fifth grade.

I once asked my mother, "Why did you want to study if nobody was supporting you in that? Her reply made  me admire her even more. She told me that she simply loved learning, even though nobody was motivating her. She dreamed of learning new things. She always says that, if she had it to do over, she would become a nurse again. I believe her because her vocation is so genuine. During the first years of the war, people couldn't go out on the street after six in the afternoon. Neighbors would come and knock gently

Photo from Rhina's mama, Francisca Majano's nursing degree, 1968.

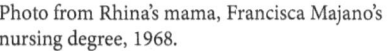

on our window to ask that my mom go with them to their house to administer an injection or connect an IV line. She always consented, though she might be dead on her feet. When the neighbors tried to pay her, she consistently refused remuneration, saying that it was not necessary, but asking that they pray that we, her children, would be blessed. My mom stockpiled a lot of blessings for my brother Stalin and me.

After my mother completed ninth grade, an opportunity arose at the National School of Nursing. She did not hesitate! She managed to get a scholarship and off she went to San Salvador to get a degree in nursing. Coming from her small town, she arrived in a big city where she wasn't familiar with anything. But little by little she learned. She has always been very enterprising and quick. She says that she went without a lot of things at first. As all she could afford was bus fare, she wore out her shoes with the extensive walking she had to do. She tells me that at times she had to put newspaper inside the soles of her shoes because they had nasty holes and she didn't have the wherewithal to buy new ones.

Laughing, she relates her adventures and misadventures during her time as a boarder at the nursing school. She says that they stole the matron's panties and hung them out like flags in the school courtyard. This mischief they visited on her because the lady was very strict with them.

My mom ended up pregnant with me while not yet married to my dad and she was very nearly denied her nursing degree.

Her situation was scandalous at the time, in 1968. She was a pregnant unmarried woman. But she went straight to find my father at the teacher training college. She arrived to inform him that she was pregnant and that they had to get married in a civil ceremony because, otherwise, she was not going to receive her diploma.

A month after her graduation, I was born, in December of the same year. They named me Rhina in honor of the doctor who attended the birth at the hospital where my mother was serving her mandatory one-year internship in the municipality of Santiago de María in the Department of Usulután. My mom says that the doctor kept coming in to cuddle me in her arms and to plead with her, "*Señora*, give me your daughter. I will raise her as my own child." My mother refused repeatedly, telling the doctor that she would absolutely not give me away. But she promised her that they would give me her name. And so, they *named* me "Rhina," rather than *surrender* me to Rhina.

When the girls were young, Mamá Rosa would not allow my mother and my aunt to have boyfriends. My mom and dad went around behind my grandmother's back. They met when my mom was only sixteen years old. My dad had been expelled from the San Salvador schools on account of his political activity. He had to go to Usulután to continue studying and by chance, wound up living in my maternal grandparents' inn. There he made my mother's acquaintance where, he said, he was instantly ⟨captivate⟩d by her, by her long black hair. They told me ⟨that⟩ the two of them were studying in different towns, far apart, each of them would walk as long as two hours to meet at a point in between. They must have been very tired from walking when they conceived me! That's why I can say, with justification, that I was brought into existence with a lot of love and "effort."

My father wrote this poem to share with me how he first fell in love with my mother:

### 1963. Your mom was at the water trough.

*"Accept this blossom, redolent of spring.*
*It bears the love I hold inside for you.*
*If the day I die finds you yet living,*
*kiss and bring it to my burial too."*
*You took it. And you lifted up your head.*
*and said you'd nothing you could give to me.*
*"What other offer could I make instead––*
*let me know, truthfully––*
*for you have my smitten soul already?"*
*If then, I am your life, receive this kiss*
*that to give to you I am sighing.*
*But do not bring it on the day I die. Return it to me now,*
*because I am already dying.*

# My Father, Guerrilla Fighter and Dreamer

He taught me my first words. He was my first teacher. He told me stories. But with my mother, he was a tyrant. Now that I am an adult, she recounts with great pain how my father was a true abuser. My mom says that one day she bought my dad some new boots. He put them on and broke them in by kicking her. My mother was a nurse. She tells it that when she used to get ready to go to the hospital for work, she had to spend a lot of time trying to hide the bruises, the evidence of the beatings that my father dealt her.

They say that once--I do not know whether it's true-- my mom went to look for my dad in a town where he was giving classes. It had been rumored that he had another woman there. My mother showed up, a pistol in her hand, shooting into the air and shouting, "That's my husband!"

She put up with him too long. But when she decided to get him out of our lives, she stood firm. It was like that song that goes:

*When a woman decides to leave / nothing on earth can make her change her mind / When a woman decides to shed her skin / she clothes herself again with a new love / When a woman decides to leave / she goes for good and never returns.[11]*

I was five years old when my mother told my father to leave the house. My father became desperate. His family sent an entourage to intervene on his behalf. My mom didn't back down. She was determined. Then he tried to commit suicide (or maybe not).

I remember that I was in the living room. I was watching cartoons on TV, eating a tortilla with mortadella. I took a piece of tortilla and then, very carefully cut the mortadella in a round, leaving a small piece in the middle for a final bite. That is what I was doing when my dad ran by. He was heading toward the bedroom where my parents slept together. Later, I remember, they carried him out bodily. They carried him as if he were unconscious. The next scene in my mind's eye is that of my mom feeding my dad spoonsfuls of soup while he lay in a hospital bed.

When I had already grown up I found out what had actually happened that day. My father had downed an entire bottle of pills in order to poison himself. Still, my mother never softened her stance. She had made her decision.

This all happened one Christmas, and since then Christmas Eves are not exactly festive for me. A gray

---

[11] *Cuando una mujer decide olvidar.* Omar Alfonso, 2018.

cloud always shows up, lightly touching my heart, and I am overtaken by a strange melancholic nostalgia. At first it doesn't make sense. Then I get it. It's the season when my dad tried to commit suicide, or maybe to manipulate my mother one more time. I adored my father. He was the one who used to carry me to bed in his arms.

My mother tells me that when my father left the hospital, she herself placed a knife and a noose in front of him and said, "Kill yourself if you want, but you are not going to live with us in this house. Your children will always be your children, but I am no longer your wife."

It takes tremendous fortitude to act the way my mother did. The love she had for my father was huge, but the decision she made was an emphatic one. Many of our neighbors condemned her obstinacy. She was now "a single woman with children." They reproached her for having friends and for going out with them to have fun. The truth is that once my dad was out of her life, my mother became a happy, fulfilled woman.

Although my grandmother labeled her "loose-living," my mom kept on living her life as she thought best. Now I

Photo of Rhina at Christmas, at the age of four. "My father took me downtown to have this photo taken. I remember walking with him, hand in hand, among the kiosks where fireworks were sold in central San Salvador."

realize that, with that attitude, she taught me one of the most valuable lessons of my life--We women can have control of our own lives.

I admired her no end. It filled me with so much pride to see her in her nurse's uniform and to know that that strong woman was my mother. I remember that every day, when it was time for her to come home from work, my brother and I would watch for her and, when she was still a ways off, we would run out of the house to welcome her with hugs. She was the center of our lives.

We were little. We adored her so much that we even invented a system whereby we could take turns sleeping close to her on alternate nights. But my little brother wanted to sleep next to her *every* night. "I'll give you one of my pupusas[12] if you let me sleep next to Mamá tonight." He was quite a clever one. He knew how to reel me in. "I'll give you my fried onions at supper." I capitulated to his tempting offers because I have always loved eating, and it didn't take much for me to relinquish my place in exchange for an extra pupusa. Even today, my mom can't believe that I traded her for a couple of "pork pupusas."

When I was small, my father treated me very tenderly. One of the first images I have of his presence is of him cradling me in his arms. Holding me in his arms, he carried me out to wonder at the colored ribbon that formed after a rain. And he said to me, excitedly, "Hijita, look at the rainbow!" Without comprehending, with my eyes I followed the movement of his arm as it pointed.

---

[12] The Salvadoran national dish. A thick, soft corn tortilla filled with meat, cheese or, other foods, that is cooked on both sides on a griddle.

Years later I came to understand that he was pointing out the bright colors in the sky.

I remember, too, the first time he took me to the kiddie park in downtown San Salvador. He lifted me onto a little train, sat me down beside him and took me by the hand. I must have been very tiny, because my dad could hardly fit in the miniature train car we were sitting in. His knees were scrunched up against the seat in front of him. But he enjoyed the train trip around the park, keeping me close to his side.

At the kiddie park in San Salvador. Rhina with her parents and her cousins, Katia and David.

I have always wondered how this individual, so sweet, changed into a violent drunk who hurt my mother. But I have also accepted that in a marriage, in those days, a male set the rules. That explains why he acted so arbitrarily and did whatever pleased him in the moment.

In El Salvador, a man assumes, rightly or wrongly, that in his home he is to be treated like a king. Given that, I understand my mother perfectly. In the long run, she stopped loving him, to the point of kicking him out of our house. She was clear, however, in that he could continue seeing us, my brother and me, whenever he wished. But he was not to come to the house intoxicated! Even with that warning, though, many times my dad came to visit us staggering drunk. I was ashamed that my friends in the neighborhood saw that my dad was a huge drunkard.

My father never understood how my mother had dissociated from him. He always grieved over how much she had once loved him. So he would tell me whenever I saw him and chatted with him on his visits.

# Cake and Communism

My father's visits, during the final years of the 1970's, were more and more infrequent. But when he did come, he would take me, sit me down beside him and tell me his incredible war stories.

He recounted, for example, that he had gone to Cuba to train as a guerrilla fighter. He said that there, kids received a really big piece of cake at snack time, upon which they shouted, "Thank you, Fidel!" With that, my dad admonished me, "You mustn't believe it when they tell you in school that Communism is bad or that Communists eat children."

I listened to his admonition, of course, but in my imagination all that arose was a big piece of cake. Later, I began to understand and considered with admiration the system in that country. I even came to the point of believing, with absolute conviction, that my guardian angel must surely be a Communist who adored tasty confections!

My dad also told me that, to get to a guerrilla encampment in the mountains, he started off at a bus station in a certain town. There he had to identify the person who would be accompanying him, helping him get him to the right place. Usually, it was children who undertook the task of being "runners"[13] during the war. My father found the boy who was waiting for him, by asking him, "Do you know where I can get crab soup?" To which the lad replied, "No. But I know where you can get *shrimp* soup." That pre-set exchange was how he confirmed that the little boy would be his guide to the area that had been liberated by the combatants, the area where the locals lived who hadn't fled but stayed to be of support to the fighters.

My dad told me that his political activity began at the age of six. Party propaganda leaflets were tucked into the waistband of his pants and his shirt down over them. He was sent to the church to wait for the parishioners to come out of Mass. Then, he was to throw all the pamphlets into the air and run from the area as fast as he could go.

So it was that my father became a member of the Communist party of El Salvador. The organization provided him with whatever he needed to get a teaching degree specializing in the social sciences and literature. They were preparing him and my aunt Vicky, his older sister, for the day when the Revolution would triumph in our country.

Tía Vicky was sent to study in the Soviet Union. When she returned to El Salvador, she fell victim immediately

---

[13] *Correos.* Child soldiers who acted as combatants, cooks, sentinels or messengers.

to persecution. One day, out of the blue, our cousin Katia arrived to stay with us in our apartment. Now that we two are adults, she tells me that they fled because the army had raided their home to capture her mother. Tía Vicky ended up in exile, and during the war, she aided her fellow countrymen who had managed to get to Nicaragua as refugees. She was a woman who always guarded the ideal of justice in her heart. And she was one of the first feminists that I know of, always blazing trails along her journey so that other woman could soar.

My dad and my aunt were consummate intellectuals. They read voraciously. My father always went around with a book under his arm, and he loved poetry. As it did for him, poetry comforts my dreams and my afternoons. As did he, I love words and the sentences they form to express ideas. I was fascinated, listening to his stories, and gradually came to understand why he was fighting.

Intrigued by the people who lead countries, I set myself to find out what profession it was that those people who became presidents studied for. I found out that many of them, such as Fidel Castro, had been lawyers. I decided then, with all of my eight years, that I too would be a lawyer, on the off chance that someday I might become the first female president of El Salvador. I so cherished that dream that I bet my brother that I would achieve it. Once, I bet him hundred colones (the national currency prior to the institution of the dollar). I still owe him, but I am not planning to pay him. Well, you never know.

My dad also taught me to sing revolutionary songs. I really liked the one that went: *My pitiable boss... he thinks I'm the poor one.*[14] My brother and I sang that song often. Once, we belted it out at the top of our lungs in the middle of the street. My mother immediately ordered us to be quiet. Anybody might have denounced us for being members or collaborators with the guerrilla forces. Or as leftists, at a minimum. This was very dangerous!

My father told me so many things about the war and his participation in it as a guerrilla fighter. He once described to me a trap they had devised and set in place on the mountain. Its purpose was literally to hunt soldiers from the army when they came to invade the region. With all the details he supplied, I could picture the situation exactly. It was a ravine, at the bottom of which they had placed a large quantity of pointed stakes. It was as if the hole harbored a giant hedgehog lying in wait. Whoever fell in would be stuck there, run through with spikes. "Just looking at the stakes," my father said, "made the hair on my arms stand on end."

I absorbed all this information, but I knew very well that I couldn't share what he was telling me with anyone. Nor could I let the cat out of the bag with any general remark such as, "My papá is a guerrilla fighter." That would have put us in a lot of danger. "The walls have ears," I was regularly warned. Children are good at picking up on the code of silence when they live in a repressive environment.

---

[14] *Pobrecito mi patrón.* Facundo Cabral, 1971.

My dad also told me once, "I'm fighting so that in El Salvador a child's dream of being a doctor won't be just a dream." Maybe the Salvadoran civil war did not eliminate poverty altogether, but without a doubt many fought and died for a just cause. We cannot forget them.

I don't understand why it was that he chose to tell *me* his stories, to share his revolutionary dreams with *me*. Perhaps somehow he knew that I was going to preserve all the family stories to retell and write them down some day. When I asked him why he didn't tell all of this to my brother, he said that when he recounted his stories I looked at him spellbound but that my brother was more interested in playing.

Despite his absence as a father, in some way he made a mark on my life by instilling in me the quest for justice and the love of poetry. Thanks to him I understood, from a little girl, that one has to fight for one's beliefs and that we must live in a way that will make the world a better place. Once, before he died, I asked him why he had fought. He thought it over, and said to me, "Because poverty had to be eradicated. I was poor. I knew what poverty was. That's why I fought."

# Growing up
## During the War

I was a strange girl, it appears, interested in strange things. To boot, I was extremely introverted and given to daydreaming.

I remember that during the nights, I would delight in listening to revolutionary songs that I had on a cassette tape. I played that on an old tape recorder of my mom's, keeping the volume really low. I learned that the revolution could also be musical!

*How sad the rain sounds on the carboard rooftops...*[15]

Whenever I listened to that song, performed by the group Los Guaraguao, I imagined the many people who had no place to live and fantasized myself protecting them from the rain. On the outskirts of the city, I had seen those huts of sheet metal and cardboard.

Mornings, before leaving for school, I hid my cassette tape under the sink in case soldiers came to search the house. Once, a magazine came into my hands that described acts of torture. My hair still stands on end when I recall that booklet. One image showed the procedure by which a person's big toe was tied tightly until it was good and

---

[15] *Techos de cartón.* Alí Rafael Primera Rosell y Los Guaraguao, 1972.

swollen with blood, and how it was then punctured with a pin. Without prior warning, the army might send soldiers into a dwelling to ransack it. We lived with that constant fear in the El Salvador of the 1980's.

We lived in what was referred to as "the educational district," an area with a lot of residents who were teachers. It was one of the locales most harassed by the government, both before and during the war. It was inhabited by thoughtful folks who analyzed everything, and condemned the repressive regime. So, they were "dangerous" persons.

My father told me that he was from the generation of teachers who had tried at first to revolutionize people's thinking, so that there would be changes in El Salvador, but that afterward, when the government launched the repression, it became necessary to fight with weapons and not merely with books.

As a little girl, I liked listening to the radio. I quite enjoyed the political speeches, although I didn't understand them completely. I could already imagine myself delivering long oral arguments in a not-too-distant future. I would stand on my bed and gesture as I made my proclamations. I would raise my arms and break into inspired tirades. I repeated phrases that I had memorized, having heard them so many times, and I stood up as if addressing an enormous crowd in some plaza somewhere. Who could have told me that one day I would become a preacher, and that my sermons, based on bible verses, would insist that the life of Jesus is a model that compels us to fight for justice?

When the war came, we learned to fear the sudden loss of our lives caused by a stray bullet or a bomb. I was panicked by the idea of dying while in a state of sin. If that were to happen, Mamá Rosa used to say, we would go to purgatory or hell, and that in both places the soul was in for immense suffering. One had to have confessed before leaving this world, and you wouldn't have exactly found me kneeling in the confessional all that often. So, when the sessions of all-night shooting started up, I couldn't sleep. I was terrified that a tracer bullet would find and kill me. I would pray the Lord's Prayer over and over. Just in case!

One afternoon—I remember it well—I was struck by that existential inquisitiveness that sometimes arrives when a person is on the threshold of adolescence. I found myself questioning whether or not God really existed. At the time, I was in fifth grade, attending school downtown in the city. Once, when my cousin Rosita and I arrived near the school, we were surprised by a horrific outbreak of shooting. All of us kids ran in the opposite direction from where we heard the shots. Rosita grabbed my hand so we could get somewhere safe. I saw a heap of garbage and belly-flopped into it to protect myself. Afterward, some locals let us into their house and gave me a drink of water to calm me down. I was extremely agitated and my breathing was irregular. That night, I begged God to forgive me for calling his existence into question. I was filled with gratitude not to have departed this word in a state of existential doubt. Abuelita had me so well-trained that I even thought the shoot-out had occurred *because* of me, to teach me a lesson on account of my disbelief.

Nights can be interminable if the only things you hear are the din of helicopters, rifle shots and machine guns. If the shooting starting during the day, I was less afraid. I felt that the light would save me from going directly to hell, that it would give me a chance to pass through the purifying antechamber of purgatory. I was truly the product of my grandmother Rosa's creation.

Abuela Rosa always sported the brown scapular of Our Lady of Mount Carmel around her neck. She used to say that, when one's time comes, the Virgin of Mount Carmel descends into purgatory to free those who wear her image on their breasts. She plucks them by the pendant on the scapular and lifts them out of purgatory as if she were fishing. I was supposed to wear one of those scapulars, just in case. But I didn't like to because it got wet when you took a bath and smelled like a moldy rag.

The experience of growing up in wartime leaves a mark on you and raises your consciousness. You learn to fight for peace. There is no point in dying riddled with stray bullets, especially without having fired a single one yourself. The brutality of the armed conflict in El Salvador made innocent victims of tens of thousands of ordinary citizens.

# The
# Community
# Hotel

The front doors of our apartment were always open to anyone who might need to stay overnight for a few days to recuperate from some ailment. We put up relations or friends who had come to the capital from the interior of the country. Ours was also a home to those of my cousins who had been rendered rolling stones as a result of the irresponsibility of my uncles.

My cousin Rosita came to live with us. My mother welcomed her. Her family couldn't support her or afford to send her for an education. I was about ten years old and she was fourteen, so my cousin became like an older sister to me. Rosita took over all the household chores. Unknown to her, of course, my cousin was following in the footsteps of my grandmother, Mamá Rosa, who had had to work from a very young age to bring home the bacon.

Rosita was fond of a certain Mexican folksong called *La basurita*, "The Little Piece of Trash." The lyrics sang, sadly, "I'm a little piece of trash blowing in the wind... like a bird flying through a desert."[16] My cousin said that was a description of her life. Once, she went and tried

---

84    [16] *La basurita*. Flor Silvestre, 1976.

to cross undocumented into the U.S. She was gone for about a month. I remember the night she came back home, emaciated and dirty from head to toe because the poor thing had not bathed in many days since she had been deported. Later, she entered the U.S. again, legally, thanks to Tía María. By dint of a lot of hard work, Rosita has managed to raise her children and now enjoys the comforts she never had in her childhood. A house of her own, for example.

On another occasion—it was during the war—we provided lodging for my cousin Nando. He was around my age and had been living with his mother, my aunt Toña, in the interior of the country, where the war was a more daily and bloody reality. Nando had lost two fingers on one hand due to the explosion of a mine. When he talked, my cousin used the archaisms common in the speech of countryfolk. For "I saw," used to say *yo* vide instead of *yo vi*. I was embarrassed for him. I had inherited the typical prejudices against hillbilly mannerisms. Without a doubt, though unknowingly, I had developed into a total city girl.

My home was always a kind of refuge. My mom offered shelter to whoever needed it. Once, a lady showed up who had murdered a man with a pistol, as far as I was able to glean from the whispering of the adults. They had just released her and she came through our house. I watched her from afar with curiosity and a certain admiration. She was young and didn't look like a murderer. She seemed more a woman carrying a burden of sorrow.

There are many abusive men, and she, perhaps, had had to defend herself.

Our apartment in the Zacamil neighborhood was small but never short of a cot that could be opened up to accommodate a visitor.

Rhina, in the arms of Tía María, with her cousins Lupita, Marina, Pacita and a friend.

# Defying
# Gender Roles

During my teen years, I rebelled against my mother. I challenged her at every turn, and she was exasperated. She didn't know what to do with me. She didn't like my neighborhood friends. She called them "slackers" and "potheads," and besides, they were older than I was. She didn't want me going out to play with them. But I went out anyway, to hang out. My grandmother took it upon herself to tell my mom that I had disobeyed her. Apparently, the entire neighborhood was whispering about my mannish attitude and my being the only female playing and spending the afternoons screwing around with the boys.

If only my mother had realized that, quite simply, I was becoming an independent woman, just like the one she was! A woman who didn't care what other people might say. But she was unable to recognize that and she was provoked by my mutinous spirit.

I was a born leader. I convinced all my male friends to follow my plans. Once, I got them to start saving up money so, at the end of the year, we could go to the big mall in San Salvador. The big attraction was to be a real delicacy, half a pizza for each of us. That was a luxury for poor neighborhood kids like us. I don't know why they paid attention to me when they were being raised to be "men." But I was the only young woman in a group of eight to ten teen males from my building, and I could stand in the midst of them and tell them what the plan was. When the day arrived and we went out, it was a resounding success. We all ate our fill of pizza. Because his father feared we would get into trouble, my friend Mauricio, "The Spider," was not allowed to go. But we brought him back his pizza, because he had also been a collaborator.

My childhood panned out entirely among boys. That's why I can't picture or bring it to mind without the presence of my brother, who was born ten months after I was. We were so close in age that he was a constant presence in all my adventures. He was my first playmate and co-mischief-maker.

My father named my brother Stalin. My father did whatever the heck he wanted. My grandfather Andrés, *Comandante Sol*, one of the first members of the Communist party in El Salvador, used to take my dad to party meetings. There my father made note of the slogans shouted by the comrades, "Long live Stalin!" "The man of steel," they called him. So, my father decided that if one day he had a son, he would be called Stalin. At home we called him "Talito" because... well... the name "Stalin" was not a common one and it was also difficult to pronounce it properly.

Stalin and I invented amazing games, such as the one where we pretended to be hens laying eggs. Bunching up the blankets, we made balls and sat on them to hatch them. Or, sometimes we made believe that we were swimming in the ocean and ran at the bed and dove onto the mattress. With merely ten months difference our ages, we were inseparable. I can't recall my childhood without him right there at my side.

Rhina's father with his schoolmates at the teacher training college.

# When I Discovered I Liked Other Girls

I believe I was about eight years old when I became aware that I was "different." A girl whom I liked to look at had stopped coming out to play, and I missed her. Then, at the age of twelve, I developed an infatuation for another girl, a neighbor named Lupita. The crush transpired unexpectedly when I saw her, began talking with her, holding her hand. Without understanding why, I fell in love for the first time, with my little friend. It was innocent play, but what a world we might have if we were only allowed to explore our inner selves without being forced into neat little boxes of gender and sexual orientation!

After getting home from school, we would visit in each other's houses and hang out talking and laughing--so much laughter--telling each other stories. Lupita had a lovely voice. I enjoyed listening to her sing the songs of The Singing Cricket[17] and Topo Gigio.[18] I still remember when she launched into Gigio's song: *Beloved Pinocchio, unforgettable toy... you were the first great love of my life.*

---

[17] *El grillito cantor,* known as Cri-Cri. A Mexican fictional character, an anthropomorphic cricket, created in 1934 by Francisco Gabilondo Soler who performed and recorded Cri-Cri's songs. Cri-Cri's popularity extended widely throughout Central America.

[18] *Topo Gigio.* Ital., "Gigio the mouse." A puppet in the form of an anthropomorphic mouse, created in 1958 by Italian artist Maria Perego. Topo Gigio has been popular in Latin America for decades, down to the present, and maintains a considerable fan base in El Salvador.

She would sing me those little songs. Her imagination was so vivid. I loved our long conversations about everything and nothing. We spent every afternoon together in our neighborhood, the Zacamil.

The feelings arose, perhaps, because we liked to hold hands, very tenderly. There was nothing indecent involved. From that, an unimaginable love, so sweet and gentle, was born. But I had no point of reference by which to give a name to what we were feeling. I had never seen another same-sex couple around me, relating in this way. And the only other person I knew who was suspected of being a lesbian was the target of rumors and gossip.

I vaguely remember that a man dressed as a woman would show up every once in a while in my neighborhood. I heard that they called her "Erika." Fascinated but apprehensive, I would secretly watch her, like something mysterious, dazzling in appearance. Erika used to dressed up nicely. She looked pretty, with her lipstick and high heels... She looked beautiful! A real trans woman, as we would say today. But I never learned her real story. I only remember the mocking whistles and catcalls directed at her by the men of the neighborhood.

Without being able to name what we were feeling, we decided to call ourselves "best friends." At the end of the afternoon, we would both begin feeling sad. We had to let go of each other. Each of us had to go off home.

When you are in love, there is never enough time. Lupita was sent around door-to-door selling cheese in the vicinity, and I would accompany her. At times, we walked around the neighborhood holding hands. Rumors concerning our strange friendship began to circulate. Lupita asked me, "Rhina, why weren't you born a boy?" I only answered with a hug.

One fine day, her father decided that we could no longer be friends. He called me and said he wanted to speak to me seriously. I remember that he said, "*Rhinita,* let's dot our i's and cross our t's." I listened, paying close attention. I liked that expression. I could imagine myself placing little dots on all the i's during our conversation. He went on to say that people were going around saying ugly things about Lupita and me, that I was probably a bad influence on his daughter, and that therefore he was absolutely forbidding our friendship. He told me that, from that day on, Lupita wasn't going to be my friend and that I should not come to see her any more in the afternoons after school.

I couldn't speak to my Lupita or go near her, for fear that she would be scolded. I learned to love her from afar, in secret. I would see her out the window when she was coming back from school, passing by my building. I had to make do with looking at her in the distance. My first heartbreak. Having my "first great love" so close became impossible. I never understood why our friendship had to end. We hadn't done anything bad to anyone. People are cruel when they simply cannot conceive of love between two women.

It was during those days, that for the first time I heard *marimacha*[19] shouted at me. That epithet hurt me so much. I knew it referred to someone unnatural, a *macha* or "manly" woman. Literally, a *María* who is *macha*. Yet, none of that succeeded in undoing my love for Lupita, and I soon came to realize that my heart held enough love still, for other girls. And living in the neighborhood was Mauricio, who, it was said, was gay. He did seem openly so. He had spent some time living in the United States and was a hair stylist. He eventually became very well known in El Salvador. We struck up a friendship.

---

[19] Pejorative colloquial term, roughly the equivalent of "dyke." A woman who by virtue of her appearance, her attitudes and behaviors would seem to be a man.

# Trying to Fit In

I must confess that, yes, I definitely tried having a boyfriend in my student years. But our courtship only lasted a couple of weeks. I just got bored. It seemed stupid to me to kiss a boy. It wasn't the same as what I felt for Lupita. With her I could spend a whole afternoon just holding her hand and that got me excited. Being with a guy just didn't do it.

Years later, when I became an evangelical Christian and was living in New York, Lupita's father consented to our resuming our friendship. So, Lupita and I started writing letters to each other, nearly every day. I kept bags full of her letters. Our correspondence was like a diary of our lives in which we told each other everything that was happening, the friends we had, the places we visited. She corrected my spelling and I really think that helped me keep my Spanish pretty much up to scratch.

My aunt and my mother opposed our friendship, characterizing it as "odd." They rummaged through my letters and found phrases of love and affection. They were of the opinion that two women should not interact that way and they told me so in angry terms.

One summer I managed to save enough money and send Lupita a plane ticket so she could come visit me in New York. I was cleaning houses with my aunt in those days. That summer stretched into a longer period of time and Lupita ended up staying in New York. Later, her dad came to join her.

I was still in love with Lupita, but she was no longer in love with me. Lupita had outgrown the infatuation of our childhood. She went on, with her father, to live in Canada where she reunited with the rest of her family who had earlier remained for a time in El Salvador.

Although I continued to feel romantic love for Lupita, I still considered it a sin since I had become a fanatical evangelical Baptist who saw nearly everything as a deviation from the holy and the pure. Dancing was sinful, listening to music was sinful, watching movies that were not Christian was sinful. How, then, could loving another woman as I did, not be a sin? In my mind and in my heart at the time, it was an *unpardonable* sin that would lead me to eternal damnation.

So began my self-imposed torture as I tried to battle myself and my sexual orientation. Many years would go by before I could accept myself as a lesbian. I prayed so hard that the attraction to other women would be lifted from me. This feeling, which was condemned from the pulpit of the church that I attended, tormented me. There were times when I offered up to God 24-hour fasts along with prayers that I be delivered from feeling attraction toward other women. But all that went through my mind while I was fasting and praying was rotisserie chickens. I thought the hours in the lead-up to midnight would never end, when I could break my fast and eat.

When I came out of the closet, I fell in love many more times. Always with women who did not reciprocate the feeling. I filled up ten diaries full of sad tales, breaking down into minute detail just how my heart was breaking, without ever understanding what real love was. Now, I reread the accounts of all my failed loves and they sound

Rhina, aged twelve, in the apartment in the Zacamil, a time when she went around with her hair uncombed and hanging in her face.

like an unending lament, as if I had been crying out to the world unceasingly, "Love me!" I had to advance a long way in order to understand that I was worthy of love, that I did not have to beg for it.

My heart needed to heal before I could learn to recognize pleasure in simple things, in the goodness that is always there. Because love doesn't have to be complicated, doesn't always have to turn one's world upside down with anxiety. *That* is how it is in the *telenovelas*, where the protagonist is involved in some slow-motion tragedy, desperately striving to get to the happy ending.

I have always considered myself an incurable romantic. I remember that, having hardly taken my first baby steps, I wobbled toward a radio on the table. It fascinated me when I put my ear up to the sound, so melodious and moving. Very soon I was hooked on songs of love and betrayal. They have been my faithful companions on countless afternoons and during walks. Even when I am at the gym, I listen to sorrowful ballads. When I was a fanatical Evangelical, I spent my time listening to Christian hymns. I delighted in the ones that sounded the most dramatic. As it turns out when poetry is what feeds you, pain is poetic.

It is strange to me how much effort goes into trying to make sense of how we grew up, so that we can cleanse our soul of everything we didn't understand at the time. I think that you just live, and everyone's stories are different, but they don't necessarily have a logical or a happy ending.

I have learned that life is a string of memories that ends up molding us, orienting us without even asking us if that is the route we want to travel. And upon traveling that particular path, lo and behold, we become who we are, human in the end, inevitably ephemeral.

True love came to me at forty-three years of age, dressed as a biracial Japanese-white woman who has made me infinitely happy. I never have to guess whether she loves me or whether I am in her thoughts. He sweetness tells me everything, and every day I learn and relearn that love can be the gentlest of breezes. This book is dedicated to her as the driving force that spurs me on.

# The Aunt Who Opened Doors

Tía María was the first to emigrate to the U.S. In El Salvador, she had tried her hand at being a seamstress, but that didn't earn her enough money and she wanted to support my mother. My father was contributing nothing to our welfare or education. My mom had to work as many as sixteen hours a day to be able to cover our household expenses. So, Tía María undertook the odyssey of millions of other Salvadorans. She told me that she had no ambitions such as obtaining property or having a large amount of money in the bank. In her mind, all she wanted to do was help her family.

Tía María departed on her journey for Houston together with a group of compatriots among whom were two of her acquaintances. She recounts that on the trip she was very despondent, that she missed "her" children, as she referred to us. She thought of us, my brother and me, and of Marina, the daughter she had unofficially adopted. As Tía tells it, when they were ready to cross the U.S.-Mexico border, the smugglers hid her and some of the others underneath a truck. One female traveling companion had long hair, and Tía held it back for her so it would not get  entangled in the wheels of the moving vehicle. Many times on the journey Tía wanted to go back, but her fellow travelers encouraged her to continue the voyage. In those moments, she could never have imagined that her brave determination would be to the benefit so many. We family members and close relations were direct beneficiaries of the arduous journey she made as an immigrant. She couldn't have known that each step she took northward would change the lives of so many people.

Tía María arrived safely in the U.S. and settled in New York in 1976. There she began to earn a living cleaning upscale homes, work that she pursued for nearly fifty years. With the earnings from that toil she helped my mother secure careers for my brother and me, and assisted many other people in getting established in the U.S. Garden City, New York, and its luxurious mansions—a neighborhood she worked in her whole life in the U.S.—knows well her reputation as an impeccable house cleaner. My aunt labored for many of its families over decades, watching their children grow up and familiarizing herself with their individual tastes. She also laundered and ironed clothes for some. And some of their floors had to be polished by hand.

In my youth, once I was in the U.S., during school vacations and in the afternoons, I accompanied her to clean houses so she would give me a little cash. The work was onerous. The vacuum cleaners were heavy. One had to clean every inch of the furniture, the bathrooms, and do the job meticulously because that is what her clients demanded. It was physically exhausting. I recall how my back ached after a day's cleaning. When she was at her best, Tía María could clean up to three houses a day. One day, when I went to visit her in Pennsylvania, where she lives currently, I asked, 'Tía, at what point in your life were you happiest?" "When I was cleaning houses," she answered. The big houses of those rich white folks owe a great deal to the humble hands of people like Tía María.

Tía María worked hard all her life. Now, she is eighty-five years old, retired, and is downhearted  because she can no longer stand up to work. She uses a wheelchair and has to be helped with all of her basic hygienic needs. But even in her wheelchair, she still makes pupusas, tamales and tortillas. The young ladies who take care of her prepare the dough and, though they are originally from the Caribbean or South America, they have learned from Tía María how to make our Salvadoran culinary specialties. Tía's knees are shot and she has also developed asthma from the chemicals she used for cleaning.

I think that deep down her answer to my question was saying, "I was happiest when I was strong and able to fend for myself." She adds that sometimes she dreams that she is cleaning houses. I can imagine that in those dreams Tía is happy because she enjoys full vitality and independence, and is able to forget the painful reality that will be waking up in a wheelchair for the rest of her days.

# Women Who
# Bestow Wings

Before leaving for the U.S., Tía María and my grandmother had been taking care of my brother and me. We were little and my mom was working long days outside of the home. My mother worked for many years in the ophthalmic clinic at Rosales Hospital in San Salvador. She was so efficient in her duties that the doctors even let her put the finishing touches on small surgeries, she tells me. Once, she brought home a small jar that held an actual eye. The neighborhood children were fascinated by it. They came to our house just to ask her to show them the glass container. The "traveling eye" quickly became an irresistible and educational attraction in the Zacamil.

When Tía departed for the U.S., my grandmother was left in complete charge of our supervision. I noticed a big change in the painstaking care we had been used to. Now we no longer looked so nice and clean and kempt. Mamá Rosa fed us, of course, be she didn't know how to show us tenderness or the individual attention that every child needs. She had never received it in her own childhood and she did not know how to provide it. Providing us with enough to survive was the baseline. Everything else was extra. In fact, she was unable to conceive of other necessities such as the need to stimulate our minds, to mold us into thinking beings. Besides, that fact that we had opinions of our own that challenged the norm filled her with fear. She used to say to me: "Clear away your brother's plate; he's finished eating." I would ask her, "Why?" "Because he's a boy," she'd retort. I didn't do it because that didn't seem a compelling enough reason for me to serve my brother.

I remember with great affection a neighbor whom I called "Tía Silvia," a woman who was very sweet to me. One day, she noticed that I was running around with my hair uncombed, hanging in my face, down over my eyes. She came, put two clips in my hair and said, "Rhinita, I bought these little butterflies so you can see, so you can play better." So, I learned to put clips in my hair.

Tía Silvia also gave me other life lessons. For example, she taught me that Hitler had perpetrated genocide. I was a strange girl. I had taken to drawing swastikas on the walls of our building. She came upon me as I was drawing one on her door. Tía Silvia called me over to talk and asked me, "Rhinita, do you know who Hitler was? "No," I said, "but on TV it looks like he's a powerful man, because the crowds praise him and salute him with their arms raised." Tía Silvia was a wise one. She made me a gift of book, the *Diary of Anne Frank* and encouraged me to read it. When I did, I realized who Hitler actually was and what had happened in the Holocaust. Tía Silvia never argued with me or forced me to think as she did. She simply gave me tools for me to use to come to my own conclusions.

One day, when my mom was going to be away for a whole weekend because she had to go to Usulután to bury my uncle Ermenegildo, Tía Silvia took me to stay overnight at her house. She went out of her way to make me feel really comfortable and on the following morning she made me hot milk with *Café Listo*.[20] I long for my Tía Silvia's gentle touch! She taught me to believe that there was goodness in me, and that, by reading, a person can acquire new knowledge and new values, and break free of ignorance.

My Tía Silvia was also my schoolteacher. My mother had decided to take me out of the school run by nuns, where I had studied up until fourth grade. She claimed that I was not learning enough and said that she wanted someone to teach me more rigorously. So, to start me in fifth grade, she put me in the hands of Tía Silvia. Tía Silvia taught classes at República de Argentina School in downtown San Salvador. I loved being her student. I learned a lot with her. She taught us how to write Roman numerals up to 10,000. She even managed to have us put on a theatrical show based on a story we had read in the yearly review. I got to play a farmer who thought he could get rich raising a hen, excited when he thought of all the eggs she would produce.

---

[20] The leading brand of instant coffee in El Salvador for over eighty years. *Café Listo* means "coffee at the ready."

I remember how much I enjoyed learning my lines and acting. For the day of the production, I got myself a pair of rancher's overalls and played my part, raising my hands up to the sky and reciting the monologue I had rehearsed with such determination. Being dramatic has been my hallmark since I was little!

Rhina's brother Stalin, Mamá Rosa, Rhina and Marina in the Zacamil, across from the building where Rhina grew up.

# My Mother Leaves for New York

In December of 1982, my mother secured a tourist visa and left to meet up with Tía María in New York. My brother and I remained at home in the care of neighbors, as Mamá Rosa had left and gone back to her town. Some nights, my grandmother Menche came to stay and take care of us.

Tía María had been covering the expenses of her daughter Marina and had also been sending money to support my brother and me. Because she stepped up, we were never in need and were able to pursue a better education in private schools. Now, my mom was leaving to go help her. Besides, it was wartime in El Salvador and no one knew how long the conflict would last.

Marina had been given into the care of Tía María soon after she was born. Her biological mother, Uncle Mere's wife, was overwhelmed with the pregnancy and with my uncle, who would not stop drinking. They say that one day she even threatened that she was going to cut her belly open to get the baby out of her. Tía came to the rescue immediately. She intercepted the knife and promised that she would adopt the baby as soon as it was born and would raise the child as her own. Thus it was that Tía María became the Marina's mother for the rest of her life.

Once Tía María obtained a green card, she returned to El Salvador to fetch Marina. Then, in 1982, my mom too left for the U.S. As soon as she arrived, she got to work cleaning houses alongside my aunt, who had already been living for several years in New York. Finally, both women decided that they would also get us to New York. My aunt undertook a trip to collect us. A week after her arrival in El Salvador she had already contracted a *coyote.*[21] I remember that the day we left El Salvador was a Sunday, and all each of us had with us was a pair of shoes, a pair of pants and a shirt with which to set off on our journey north.

My mom had never spoken to us about any plan for all of us to go to the U.S. When she left El Salvador she had never mentioned to my brother or me, when she left, that she had no plan to return, and that a few months after her departure she would send to have us brought to join her. That is how a lot of things were decided in my family, without soliciting our opinion, without talking over what those decisions might mean. All we could do was simply trust that my mother and my aunt knew what was best for us.

---

[21] A guide for would-be immigrants to the U.S. A human smuggler. *Coyotes* are known for often being unscrupulous, exploitative and cruel to the persons who engage their assistance.

# Little Wetbacks,
# Wet but Worthy

So, we left. As if on an excursion that was going to last a whole month. We traveled in the company of a group of twenty individuals. I remember that one family's children were excited at the idea of going to Disneyland. But their parents hushed them constantly because they didn't want it known that we were going to cross into the U.S. illegally.

When we got to Tijuana, all of us together were put in a safe house. The *coyote* who had transported us from El Salvador said that he would go wash our clothes, since we couldn't go out. The minute he left, the Mexican federal police, the *federales*, descended upon us and arrested us. It's funny, because at that very moment we had been practicing singing the Mexican national anthem! We had to pass as Mexicans while we were on Mexican territory.

The police brought us to a cell that had one tiny window that looked out onto the street. I remember feeling despair at having been locked up in a dark, dirty cell, able only to look outside through the tiny window, wanting badly to be set free. After threatening to return us to our home country, the *federales* told us that, if we paid them, they themselves would pass us on to another group of *coyotes*. And that is how we got ourselves released.

These other *coyotes* were Mexicans. They threatened us too. Every other minute they were warning us not to try to escape because they were being sought on both sides of the border for having killed people. They held us in a room with mattresses on the floor. It was dreadful being there. We felt like animals.

On our first attempt to cross the border, I suffered the bitterest cold of my life, to the point that my teeth were chattering. The *coyotes* ordered us to lie down on the grassy ground. They kept a lookout, waiting for the moment that the gringo border patrol withdrew, so we could attempt the crossing. While we were lying on our stomachs, the wet, frozen ground penetrated my body to the bone. I peed my pants. I was shivering with the icy cold. Never in my life have I felt anything like it. Well, perhaps I have... when discrimination feels as piercing cold past bearing.

When we had finally crossed, we made our way, in silence, over mountains, down sidewalks. We had been walking several hours when the coyotes shouted for us to hide. Now we had the border patrol on top of us! In a matter of seconds, a helicopter appeared––they called it *el mosco*, "the mosquito"––shining down bright light on the entire area as if it were daytime.

The *gringo* police ordered us to come out of hiding, one by one. I was holed up under a bush with my aunt. My brother had climbed a tree, but says that, when he saw that we two had been caught, he decided to come down and hand himself over. Stalin was irritated with us because we hadn't hidden well enough. The U.S. immigration agents began interrogating us. We told them that we were Mexicans. In those days, forty years ago, they didn't know how to distinguish between different groups of immigrants.

We were all put in a van to spend the night. They didn't give us water or let us use the bathroom. I remember that a lady in our group vomited during that inhumane imprisonment in the van.

It was strange to be there. I felt like I was out of my body. It seemed as if I were looking down from above on everything that was happening, as if it were a movie.

The following day, they threw us out, back on the other side of the border in Tijuana. That's when my aunt María rolled up her sleeves. Off she went to look for another way for us to cross the border again. She sent to my mother in New York, asking for more money, and negotiated our transfer to yet other group of *coyotes*. I don't know what she did or how she did it, but she did *something*. I believe that first she had to pay the ones we were then with to let us go, and then she had to entrust our lives to the new ones. While she was conferring with the gangsters who were holding us, I was really afraid, worried that if something happened to her, we would no longer have anyone to protect us.

Having been transferred to the third group of *coyotes*, that same night we repeated our attempt to cross the border. We were walking along a highway when the Mexican federal police intercepted us again. Once more, they took us to the station, and again we had to pay them in order for them to release us.

The *federales* themselves then led us to a sewage outflow culvert that opened right at foot of the chain-link fence that ran along the border. The boundary we crossed forty years ago doesn't look anything like the concrete wall you see today. We walked for what seemed a half hour. They gestured for us to lie down on the grass near a highway. Shortly thereafter, some cars appeared. We were told to get in and, in a few minutes, we were in San Diego.

We disembarked at a safe house for immigrants who had recently crossed. And there was my aunt, waiting for us. That last leg of the journey my brother and I had made alone. Inside at the safe house, my aunt had lit a candle and, together, she and I went to give thanks to God. Later, she cooked me an egg with Kraft yellow American cheese, the first thing I ate in the United States of America!

# Negotiating
## with God

When, in that moment of desperation, my aunt had plucked up the courage to look for another solution to crossing the border, the *coyotes* had taken her aside. I was terrified because I thought something might happen to her, and I went out to a courtyard, knelt and began to pray the Lord's Prayer.

Later on, I would start negotiating, as they say, with God. I promised him that, if we managed to exit that nightmare safely, I would return to church, would go back to hearing Mass and going to Confession. I would be a good person. To be honest, I had long since stopped observing all of those things. I was fourteen years old and had become quite rebellious. But in that difficult moment, I asked God with all my heart to save us in exchange for my promise to be a better believer. Once I had gotten established in New York, I wanted to fulfill my promise. But that is another story, and I will tell it further on.

Returning to the matter at hand: finally, we arrived in Los Angeles. From there, in a Lincoln Continental we resumed the trip in the company of the other family who had crossed the border with us. They too were heading for New York. We were about twelve people, crammed into that car, and our journey overland took three days.

My overjoyed mother was waiting for us in the backyard of the house where she was living. I was every bit as happy, now that we were no longer hiding or fleeing. She and my aunt were renting two rooms in the dark, dank basement of the house. That first night in New York I missed my apartment in the Zacamil. I told my mom that night, "I want my little bed, my little house, my litte pillow." We were together now and that was the most important thing, she countered.

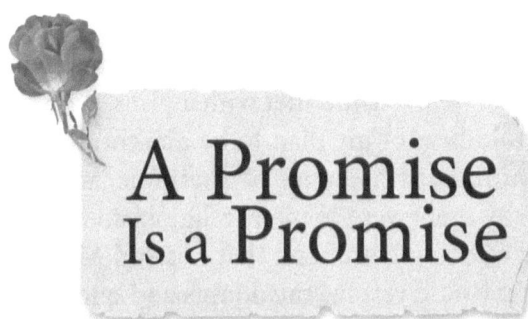

# A Promise
## Is a Promise

I tried. And I truly did want to fulfill my promise to God when I arrived in New York. I went to a church close to where we lived and met with a priest who spoke Spanish. I told him of my plan to be a faithful believer. But I told him that I had a lot of questions, and one of them was why there were so many religions in the world. His answer was to recommend that I attend Mass every Sunday. That would resolve my doubts and questions.

As fate would have it, we moved from the basement, where we were living after our recent arrival, to an apartment complex right next to a Baptist church that I could see out our window. Once, I glimpsed a teacher from my bilingual studies program go in, and the next day I asked her what one had to do to attend that church. One day, I passed through the doors and I stayed until I was twenty-six years old, when, finally, I came out of the closet.

I became a fanatic and homophobic evangelical Christian. I went out to canvass bus stations, to evangelize on Saturday mornings. I tried to convert people to the form of Christianity that I was practicing, and, as I have always been audacious, I would approach them sternly, "Have you accepted Jesus as your Lord and Savior? Repent!" I have always said that my first job as a community organizer was my mission to save souls from hell!

In that church, at the age of nineteen, I married a Salvadoran man from Morazán. He was a good man and was by my side during the years when I was studying to become an attorney. He always believed that I would accomplish it. Whenever I had to take a difficult exam, we would pray together. The truth is, with him experienced a lot of personal growth. But little by little I was realizing that the life I was living was not the one I wanted to live. I remember that at times, when I was at the university, I would felt like I was another Rhina, different from the one who passed through the doors of the church and uttered long prayers of contrition. It was as if I were living a double life, one as an independent woman and one as a woman who was a slave to dogma.

At the age of twenty-six, I could tolerate it no longer. I sat down to have a talk with the man who was then my husband and I told him, "When I embrace you, I am really wanting to embrace a woman." As a good Christian couple, we turned to prayer, looking for direction. We decided that we would seek counsel. But it had to be from a Christian like ourselves, so that this person would not lead us astray. We were lucky, because we found a pastor who was not *only* a pastor but a clinical psychologist as well. That fine man helped me recognize that I was not possessed by any demon, that what I was experiencing was as human as being heterosexual.

I recall that he asked me what it was that attracted me in a woman. I told him that it was intelligence, tenderness, empathy. And that the other person *was* a woman and not a man. He looked at me and said, "See? I didn't fall out of my chair. That's because nothing you said surprised me or made me jump out of my skin." In him I saw reflected as in a mirror the acceptance of who I was, a woman who was simply attracted to other women.

On our seventh wedding anniversary, we decided to separate. We began dividing up what we owned. Knowing that in the church we had been seen as an exemplary couple, and that we had important leadership roles there, we spoke with the pastor and the deacons. Although we didn't explain the specific reason for which we were separating, rumors had already begun to spread. It was an open secret. The pastor looked at me pointedly and said, "Have you considered eternity?" I don't know how I managed to respond, but I did, that the only thing I planned to do was trust in divine grace. That church, which had been my refuge as an immigrant, became a place where the judgmental stares no longer allowed me to enter. I lost a part of myself. I took refuge in my work as a labor law attorney at an immigrant worker center. There I spent my time, even on weekends, calculating the wages owed to landscapers, construction workers, housekeepers. When we occasionally won in court, but the employer insisted on not paying up, we went to his home or business to protest, using public shaming to make him compensate his workers.

In 1999, I took my first trip to El Salvador as part of a delegation for the purpose of observing the presidential election of that year because the FMLN[22] was then running, for the first time, as a political party. I had come to El Salvador before, but those were always family or tourist visits. Never before had I visited for the purpose of conducting an analytical assessment of the country. That trip made its impression on me and when the opportunity came up to work for the SHARE Foundation,[23] I applied for the position.

I moved from New York to California to take the job, and I left the practice of law to become a community organizer. My role consisted of identifying Salvadorans like me who had left in the 1980's and who wanted to reconnect with their native country and to participate in its development. When the earthquake hit in 2001,[24] the base of Salvadorans that I had helped organize raised funds to assist.

After moving to California, I also began attending seminary. I didn't want to be a pastor. I simply wanted to return to formal education, and this was a field of study that interested me. As I studied for my Masters in Theology, I came to understand the expansiveness of the divine and in that context, I was able to reconcile my Christian identity with my sexual orientation.

---

[22] The leftist *Frente Farabundo Martí para la Liberación Nacional*, the Farabundo Martí front for National Liberation, known familiarly as the *Frente*, founded in El Salvador in October of 1980.
[23] Salvadoran Humanitarian Aid, Research and Education Foundation, founded in 1981, with offices in San Salvador and the San Francisco Bay Area. The Mission of the SHARE Foundation is to strengthen solidarity among the Salvadoran people in El Salvador and the United States in the struggle for economic sustainability, justice, and human and civil rights.
[24] On January 13, 2001 a massive 7.7 magnitude earthquake struck El Salvador.

When the funds that supported my post at the SHARE Foundation ran out, I started working in the area of domestic violence prevention. I initiated a program for community leaders to combat domestic violence. Because my leaders and I held hands and sang songs together, my boss told me that my meetings seemed more like religious services. I started to think about the idea of becoming a pastor. But the thought of being a religious leader terrified me. All I knew about such leaders was that they seemed infallible and unwavering in their faith. That wasn't me. I had doubts about faith and I often made mistakes.

I started attending a church that had two female pastors as its leaders, one white and one black. They manifested to me the female side of God, and little by little I was able to see that it is possible to lead from a place of vulnerability and humility. They laid out a path for me to begin my process of ordination. Although I had already received my Masters in Theology, it would take five more years to complete the requirements of ordination in the United Church of Christ (UCC). The day of my ordination was one of the happiest days of my life. I was led into the church held by the hands of my two pastors, I received my investiture as a minister of the Word and presided over my first Communion table. It was a dream come true. I remember that, when I was little, every time the priests celebrated Communion and the little bells rang at the consecration, I would ask Jesus to enter into my heart as he was the elements of bread and wine. This time it was I who was leading that ritual, and I could have died satisfied in that moment. Life had made plain to me why I had come into this world.

So it was that I founded a small faith community— *Ministerio Latino*—that for twelve years has been home to many LGBTQI+ individuals, helping them recover and reclaim their Christian faith. It was my goal that this safe place would exist for my queer siblings. It's a small community, but tens of individuals have come through, people who had no idea that God still loved them, though many others had told them that was not the case. How many stories there are of people who have spent years not hearing the hymns they learned in their childhood because they "had to" forget them when they came out of the closet.

My work in the UCC has been precisely that of opening the doors to more people who, like me, were exiled from their churches. We don't deny Communion to anyone, and I have baptized trans siblings with the new names that correspond to their gender expression. I could never have imagined that young girl who condemned everything would now embrace everything.

Since 2018, through *Ministerio Latino*, I have been bringing various activists and U.S. faith leaders to El Salvador to form bonds of collaboration with human rights organizations that work for the advancement of the LGBTQI+ community, or who are interested in protecting the environment. It is also important to me that these visitors get to know our history of struggle and faith, that they know our martyrs, that they know that the spirit of Monsignor Romero[25] continues to infuse us with hope.

---

[25] Óscar Arnulfo Romero y Galdámez (1917–1980), a prelate in the Catholic Church in El Salvador. His last position was as auxiliary bishop of San Salvador. A tireless advocate of social justice, he was assassinated by a right-wing death squad while in the act of celebrating Mass. He was officially canonized by the Catholic Church on October 14, 2018, as Saint Oscar Romero.

For me, in particular, these trips have served to ground me. They remind me that I left a place of which I am extremely proud. That in my heart there is a volcano that, though dormant, holds fire.

I wanted to immortalize all of these stories because though they are unique, they are the stories of many of us who grew up in a land of dreams in a time of repression. They are the extraordinary stories of an ordinary family, like many others in El Salvador. They are family stories that have rattled around in my head for more than fifty years, dogging me, desirous of making it onto paper so that they could be told. They are the stories that my grandmother Mamá Rosa can no longer chase after me to erase.

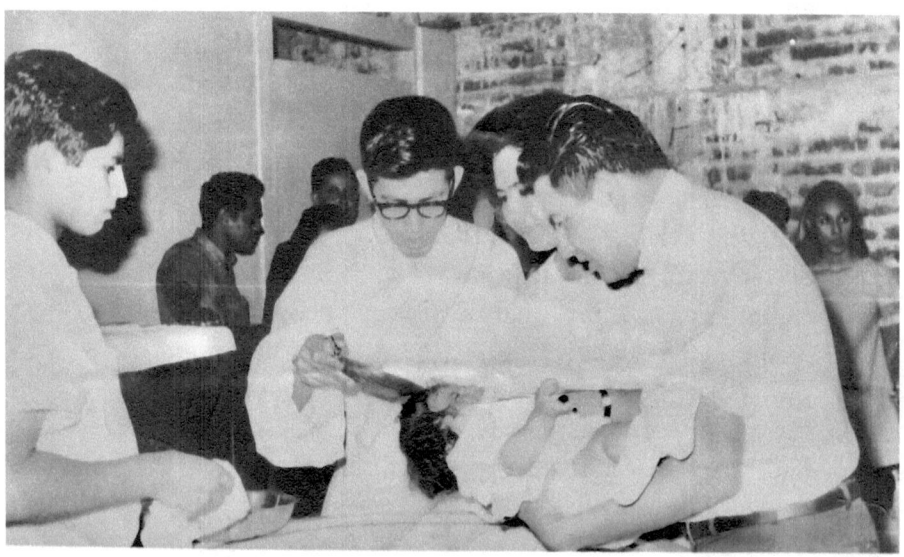

The day Rhina was baptized in San Salvador cathedral. Julián Ortega and Ángela Najarro, godparents.

# Glossary of Spanish Language Terms Used in the Text

| | |
|---|---|
| Abuela | grandmother |
| Abuelita | grandma, granny |
| Abuelo | grandfather |
| Abuelito | grandpa, granddad |
| Gringo/a | English-speaking Anglo-American |
| Federales | Mexican national police |
| Hija, hijita | daughter |
| Mamá | mamma, mother, mom |
| Ojo de Dios | eye of God |
| Papá | father, dad |
| Tía | aunt, auntie |
| Tío | uncle |

# About the Author

Rhina Mercedes was born in Santiago de María, Usulután on December 14, 1968. Her parents were Francisca Majano Flores and José Orlando Rodríguez Cortéz. As a consequence of her migration to the U.S., she acquired the surname Ramos.

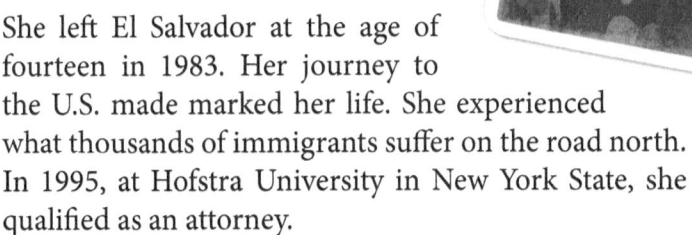

She left El Salvador at the age of fourteen in 1983. Her journey to the U.S. made marked her life. She experienced what thousands of immigrants suffer on the road north. In 1995, at Hofstra University in New York State, she qualified as an attorney.

In 2003, she obtained a Masters in Theology from the Pacific School of Religion. In 2012, she founded a community of faith under the auspices of the United Church of Christ specifically purposed to welcome LGBTQI+ individuals who had been excluded from other churches.

Rhina Mercedes resides in California, where, as a Latin American woman, she vigorously preserves her cultural roots.

# About the Publisher

Riot of Roses Publishing House was founded in 2021 specifically to amplify the stories of historically silenced voices and narratives.

Xicana owned. Mujerista focused. For the people.

We publish books that heal and liberate.

Read our rebellion.

Find & follow us @riotofrosespublishing

Visit us at www.riotofrosespublishinghouse.com

**RIOT OF ROSES**
PUBLISHING HOUSE
SEJATNGA
UNCEDED TONGVA TERRITORY
SOUTH WHITTIER, CALIFORNIA